The Library of the PILGRIMS

Plymouth: *Surviving the First Winter*

Susan Whitehurst

The Rosen Publishing Group's
PowerKids Press™
New York

To Savannah, who can now read my books

Published in 2002 by The Rosen Publishing Group, Inc.
29 East 21st Street, New York, NY 10010

First Edition

Book Design: Maria E. Melendez
Project Editor: Frances E. Ruffin

Photo Credits: Title page (all) © Bettmann/CORBIS; pp. 4, 7, 8, 10, 11, 12, 15, 20, 22 © North Wind Pictures; pp. 14, 17, 18, 19 © Museum of London; p. 16 © The Granger Collection.

Whitehurst, Susan.
Plymouth : surviving the first winter / Susan Whitehurst.— 1st ed.
    p. cm. — (The library of the Pilgrims)
ISBN 0-8239-5809-4 (lib. bdg.)
1. Pilgrims (New Plymouth Colony)—Social life and customs—Juvenile literature. 2. Pilgrims (New Plymouth Colony)—Social conditions—Juvenile literature. 3. Massachusetts—History—New Plymouth, 1620–1691—Juvenile literature. 4. Massachusetts–Social conditions—17th century—Juvenile literature. 5. Massachusetts—Social life and customs—To 1775—Juvenile literature. [1. Pilgrims (New Plymouth Colony) 2. Mayflower (Ship) 3. Massachusetts—History—New Plymouth, 1620–1691.] I. Title.
F68 .W595 2002
974.4'02—dc21

00-013034

Manufactured in the United States of America

Contents

A Cold Cape Cod

In November 1620, the 102 passengers of the *Mayflower* sat in Cape Cod Bay and wondered what to do next. The *Mayflower* and her Pilgrims had left England late in September and had traveled stormy seas to Massachusetts. They had been given permission to start a **colony** in Virginia. If it had been summer, the *Mayflower* might have been able to sail down the coast to Virginia. Instead, the Pilgrims faced the winter and freezing cold in Cape Cod. They had to find a place to live, and quick.

The Pilgrims were worn out by their long trip, and they were running out of food. Captain Christopher Jones wanted to sail the Mayflower back to England.

◄ *The Pilgrims were met with bitter cold weather when the Mayflower landed in Massachusetts.*

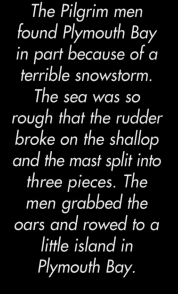

The Pilgrim men found Plymouth Bay in part because of a terrible snowstorm. The sea was so rough that the rudder broke on the shallop and the mast split into three pieces. The men grabbed the oars and rowed to a little island in Plymouth Bay.

Finding a New Home

Before the Pilgrims could explore the land and waterways near their landing spot, they had to repair the **shallop**. They needed the small boat to explore the coast of Cape Cod. While the men were fixing the boat, the women and children went ashore to do the laundry. Their clothes hadn't been washed in more than two months. As the clothes dried on nearby bushes, the children ran up and down the beach. For almost a month, the Pilgrim men looked for a place to build their colony. On December 9, they rowed to a little island in Plymouth Bay.

This hand-colored woodcut is a view of the shoreline at Plymouth colony in Cape Cod. ▶

The Pilgrims Find Plymouth

On December 11, 1620, 10 Pilgrim men rowed across a bay and explored the land. Captain John Smith had discovered the area six years before and had named it Plymouth, after a town in England. There was a harbor for ships, trees for wood to build houses, a brook for water, and a hill. Captain Myles Standish, the Pilgrims' only soldier, said the hill would be a good place for building a fort. The ocean was full of fish. Ducks and geese swam in the stream. Best of all, Plymouth was a deserted Native American village and some of the land had been cleared to plant crops.

◄ *This is a portrait of Captain Myles Standish, who sailed on the Mayflower and was the only soldier in Plymouth.*

The Native Americans, who had lived in Plymouth, had all died in 1617 of smallpox. It is believed that they may have caught the disease from English fishermen who visited the area before the Pilgrims.

The wind blew so hard that Captain Jones had to put three anchors down to keep the Mayflower (above) from blowing out to sea after landing in Plymouth.

The *Mayflower* Stays

The *Mayflower* sailed into Plymouth Harbor in December 1620. On board were 35 passengers known as **Separatists**. They wanted to practice their religion freely. There were another 67 people who were farmers and **tradesmen** and their families.

The women and children stayed on the unheated *Mayflower* while the men worked to build houses in Plymouth. At night the men would go "home" to the *Mayflower*. As the winter weather grew worse, the Pilgrims suffered from cold and wet and hunger. Their clothes got wet and there was no way to dry them. They had to wear cold, soggy clothes.

This is a map of Plymouth Harbor that shows where the Pilgrims started their colony. ▶

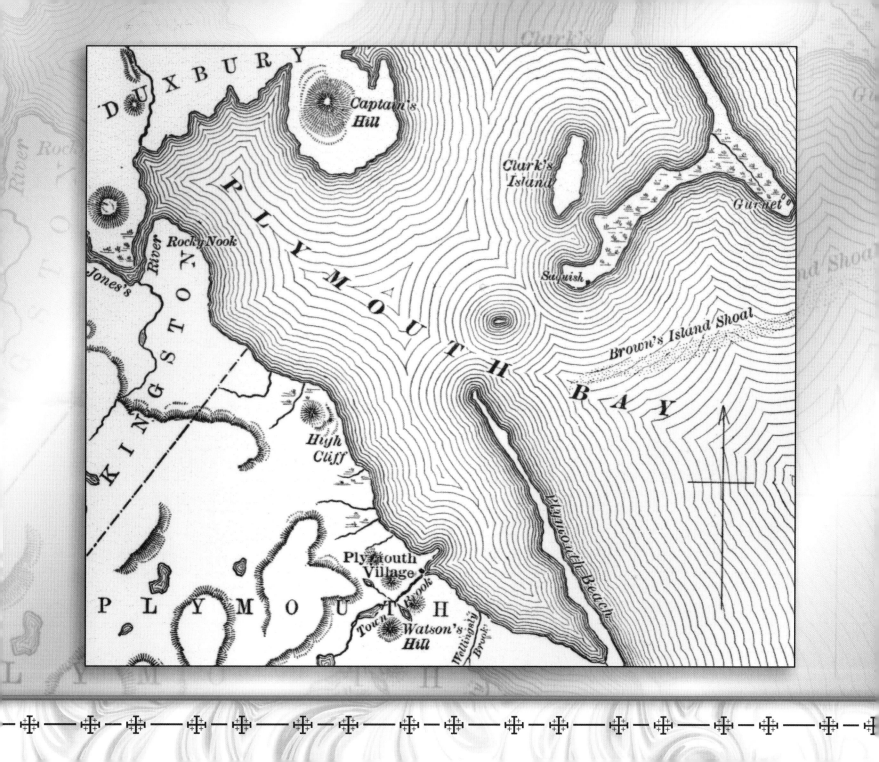

A Street and a Beginning

Once they came ashore, the Pilgrims planned how to lay out their town. Building began on December 23. Work stopped only on Sundays for church services, which lasted all day. The Pilgrims made one street that began at the top of the hill and ran to the beach. It was called The Street. Each family was given a plot of land along The Street for a one-room house and a garden. Each house was home to a whole family, plus a few unmarried men who lived with them. The first house the Pilgrims built in Plymouth was called the common house.

The Pilgrims are shown attending the first church in New England. Church services lasted all day on Sundays.

To build the common house, the Pilgrims chopped down trees and sawed them into wooden planks. Wooden pegs, made by the boys, were used instead of nails. The floor was packed dirt. The roof was thatch, dried grass tied into bundles. The common house was supposed to be a storehouse, but it soon became a hospital.

The jar shown here is a Netherlands Majolica drug jar. It's thought to have been used to carry medicine on the Mayflower. There wasn't enough medicine to fight all of the illnesses the Pilgrims suffered in Plymouth.

Hunger and Sickness

The Pilgrims had to live on the food that was left over from their long voyage. They couldn't plant crops in the frozen dirt. Their fishing hooks were too large to catch the fish in the stream. Their **muskets** were so loud that one shot scared away all the animals. There was fresh water for drinking, though, and they found shellfish and nuts to eat. Every now and then, someone would catch a duck or shoot a deer. The Pilgrims hadn't tasted fresh fruits or vegetables for months. Soon almost all of the Pilgrims were sick. William Bradford wrote a book called *Of Plymouth Plantation*. He called this time the Great Sickness.

The hungry settlers tried to hunt with their muskets for deer and wild turkeys. ▶

Difficult Times

Some days there were only a few Pilgrims who were well enough to care for the sick. The healthy ones gathered firewood and made fires. They cooked for the sick people, washed them, and made their beds. William Bradford wrote that they took care of the sick day and night, willingly and cheerfully, out of true love for their friends. The sickness was so great that often two or three people would die in one day. The healthy people were weak from hunger.

This is an example of a water bottle used by travelers in the seventeenth century. Water bottles like these were carried and used by the Pilgrims on the Mayflower.

During their first winter in Plymouth, the Pilgrims suffered many different illnesses. The colony had only one doctor, and the Pilgrims used herbs for medicine.

This pewter bottle with a screw-on top was the kind of bottle Pilgrim mothers used for feeding their babies on the *Mayflower* and at Plymouth colony.

Fewer Than Half Survive

About half of the 102 Pilgrims who had arrived on the *Mayflower* died during the first winter in Plymouth. Only four of the 18 women who had sailed from England on the *Mayflower* **survived**. Half the married men lived, and 19 of the 29 unmarried men lived. Four entire families were wiped out, and only three married couples made it through the winter together.

Most of the children lived, however. That included all seven girls and 10 of the 13 boys. The Pilgrims must have given their children the best food and the warmest clothes.

A young Pilgrim boy might have worn a leather jerkin, or sleeveless jacket, with "pinked" or punched decorations like the one shown here. Leather garments offered protection and warmth.

Spring Comes Early

In 1621, the Pilgrims were thankful that spring had come early. William Bradford wrote that the weather in March of that year was warm and fair, and the birds sang in the woods. The Pilgrims realized that they had made it. Even though they were thin and dressed in rags, they had survived against impossible odds. Plymouth colony was beginning to take shape. Seven houses had been completed. People began to feel healthier and stronger. The warm weather brought new hope. Now was the time to build more houses and to plant crops.

◀ *The Plymouth wilderness was filled with deer.*

By springtime, the Pilgrims were feeling much better. When the Mayflower sailed out of Plymouth Harbor on April 5, 1621, not a single Pilgrim chose to go back to England.

Like the Pilgrims, Plymouth Rock has had a tough time. The people of Plymouth moved the rock around town four times between 1774 and 1920. It was broken in half twice. Before it was given a safe home, visitors often chipped off pieces to take home a part of American history.

The Rock and the Spirit

Did the Pilgrims really step onto Plymouth Rock? Was that their first step onto American soil? It may have been. Plymouth Rock would have been a fine place to land the shallop. The Pilgrims never mentioned the rock in their letters and diaries, so no one knows for sure. What Americans do know is that Plymouth Rock is an important **symbol** of the Pilgrims' bold spirit. Today Plymouth Rock sits in Plymouth Bay waiting for the thousands of visitors who come each year. It is much smaller now than when the Pilgrims first saw it. Still, we remember that Plymouth Rock welcomed the Pilgrims to a new land, a new adventure, and a new nation.

Glossary

colony (KAH-luh-nee) A group of people who leave their country to settle in another land.

muskets (MUS-kits) Guns with long barrels used in battle and in hunting.

Separatists (SEH-puh-ruh-tists) People who belonged to a religious group that wanted to separate from the Church of England.

shallop (SHAH-lup) A small boat that has sails or is rowed in shallow waters.

survived (sur-VYVD) To have stayed alive.

symbol (SIM-bul) An object or design that stands for something important.

tradesmen (TRAYDZ-men) Workers who are skilled at certain jobs.

Index

B
Bradford, William, 14, 17, 21

C
Cape Cod, 5, 6
children, 6, 10, 18
church services, 13
clothes, 6, 10, 18
cold, 5, 10
common house, 13
crops, 9, 14, 21

E
England, 5, 9, 18

F
food, 14, 18

H
house(s), 10, 13, 21
hunger, 10, 17

M
Mayflower, 5, 10, 18

O
Of Plymouth Plantation, 14

P
Plymouth Rock, 22

S
Separatists, 10
shallop, 6
sick, 14, 17
Smith, Captain John, 9
Standish, Captain Miles, 9
Street, The, 13

V
Virginia, 5

W
weather, 10, 21

Web Sites

To learn more about the Pilgrims at Plymouth, check out these Web sites:
www.kidinfo.com/American_history/colonization_Plymouth.html
www.plimoth.org